Thrive Under Pressure

The Ultimate Tips and Techniques for Performing Well Under the Gun and Using Pressure Situations to Your Advantage to Rise to the Top

I0425365

Table of Contents

Introduction

Sweaty palms, knotted tongue, and a heart that's about to jump out of your chest. Finding the right words - or any words for that matter - seems like an impossible challenge. Does this ring a bell? If you cannot keep your cool when the stakes are high and you are unable to perform as per your own or others' expectations, then you have definitely landed at the right place.

Thriving under pressure is a rare quality which not everyone possesses. But it is indeed possible to acquire it overtime, and this book is here to prove that point. With the right frame of mind aided with the right skill set, this art can be learnt by virtually anybody.

But no matter how much knowledge you gather, if that knowledge doesn't help you to practically solve your problem, then there is no use to it. And like all other self-help books, this book will help you to thrive in pressure situations with the help of two things; i) An approach i.e how to view them as opportunities ii) Practical steps which can be used to excel in both your professional and personal lives.

By the end of this book you can overcome your fear of failing in crunch times and see the opportunity in adversity in order to deliver a successful performance. Knowing how to approach the task with the right mindset guarantees that you're halfway done overcoming those pressure situations.

Whether at your workplace, at home, or running track at the gym, no matter what your pressure may be, the tips in this book will help you pull the impossible challenge by the root in order to allow yourself to blossom.

Want to learn how to move past the awkwardness when staring at a pressure situation? Read on to challenge your mind and see yourself work your way to the top.

The Psychology of Pressure

Pressure is an inevitable part of life. Whether working against the clock to submit a work project and meet the deadline, pushing your body to run 10 miles so you can prepare for a marathon, or simply making sure that the dinner you're preparing for your in-laws turns out to be perfect, most of us bump into pressure situations on a daily basis. When the bar is high, intimidation swoops in and feelings of fearful nature overcome us. What if I don't meet the deadline? What if I fail to impress my mother in law?

We all deal with inconveniently challenging situations regularly, but how many of us do actually rise to the occasion? Whether you like it or not, it's all in your mind. What gives pressure to the situations you find uncomfortable? Your thoughts and feelings, of course. The way you feel about given moments determines whether you will succeed at the task at hand or not. It all depends on your mental approach towards the situations.

Most of us are inclined to play things safe and stay within the lines of our comfort zone. Once we are pushed over those lines, we feel fearful and anxious, worrying if we have got what it takes to find our way back to safety. But greatness is almost never found in our safely walled-in worlds. It is actually hiding behind those uncertain, high-pressure situations, patiently waiting to be unleashed. Plus pressure is something which makes our lives livable.

Imagine a life without all the pressure and challenges it generally comes with. That would be no life. Everything would be too easy and dull. Obviously, people strive towards a life which is free of all the unexpected twists and turns. Getting there requires going through a storm of problems you never fancied in the first place. That is what makes you cherish the journey the most. Think of pressure as your much needed pinch of spice in a relatively tasteless dish.

To paint you a picture, take an example of my friend Harris. Harris is one of those people who just likes to have everything in order. He doesn't like surprises and tends to do his best to avoid them whenever possible. You know like, knowing the weather forecast in advance, preparing work clothes the night before, packing a few extra essentials in a backpack when going on a trip just in case, and things of that sort. No, he is not obsessive-compulsive, but he is just comfortable with being familiar with the situation and does not cope well with uncertainties.

One time, Harris was given an opportunity to work alongside another friend on a project to earn a commission. The work was not in Harris' expertise, but he could have easily learnt the job if he invested some of his personal time. Afraid of the uncertain outcome of trying something new and doubting whether he would actually be able to complete the job, Harris turned down the opportunity thinking if he is not gaining anything he is not losing either. That was where he was wrong. It wasn't a couple of months after that, that his boss at work assigned a similar project to him. The project was really important for the firm. But since Harris thought he was doing 'Okay' with his current set of skills and didn't need to add new ones in the first place, he struggled and eventually the project was assigned to someone else.

So, what is my point here exactly? Pressure is inevitable. And there is no chance you can avoid it. Your only option is to embrace it with open arms at the earliest. Because sooner or later those moments will come back and test you again. Had Harris accepted his friend's project two months earlier, he would have not only been familiar with that sort of work, but also much more comfortable with the pressure that the situation brought upon him at work. You see, leaving your comfort zone does not only help you try something new but also equips you with a better mindset when similar pressure situations come across your way.

Why We Choke Under Pressure

You may have the best and brightest ideas for a new work project, but if you find the competition intimidating and let the importance of the meeting overwhelm you, you may find yourself unable to speak, let alone present your thoughts. Choking under pressure is a common occurrence for most people. But why does it occur?

In order to understand the neuroscience behind choking under pressure, let's first see what happens when we are performing a simple activity.

Imagine you're hanging out with friends on a weekend. Everybody is talking and laughing and having a good time. You are even cracking jokes and engaging in friendly banter. Here talking comes naturally to you and you don't think how you look while you're talking.

Now imagine you have been tasked with presenting an annual performance report to the Board of Directors of your company. Your entire department is counting on you to make sure you highlight all the important tasks which were done previously. Do you think talking will come naturally in this case? I don't think so. Here, you will probably think about each and every word you utter in order to leave a lasting impression on the board.

Unfortunately, the more we think about the performance of a task, the more confused we get, and the higher the chance for failure. Which is why something as simple as talking seems weird when we have to do it in front of a lot of important people.

This happens because instead of using the subconscious part of the brain (which we use when talking to a group of friends), we start using the conscious part and begin overthinking the situation, which is when the choking begins.

This conscious process expends an enormous amount of energy and ends up depleting us of the healthy focus we need in order to succeed. That leads to impaired performance, or in other words, that's the reason why we choke when faced with a high-pressure situation.

It takes some work and effort in order to prepare the mind and get it into the right state, but with time using the best techniques in order to perform well under pressure and you will never have to choke ever again.

Do not Survive, Thrive!

If you own a pressure cooker or know how to handle one, then you can understand how much your mind is similar to pressure cookers when it is under pressure. If not handled with care, the pressure cooker can be a dangerous appliance. If the steam is not released properly, the pressure can pile up inside up to the point of explosion. Besides the fact that your dinner can easily become the new paint for your kitchen, a hand injury is most likely guaranteed. But, if you handle it properly, the pressure cooker can provide you with the juiciest and most delicious meals with almost no hassle involved.

A pressure situation, if not approached with the right mindset, can also do you harm. If you do not learn how to handle the situation properly, you will keep adding negative thoughts to your mind, the same way you apply pressure to the pressure cooker. If you do not release those thoughts the right way, there is only so much energy that your mind can support. Although your mind will not explode in the literal sense of the word, piling up negative pressure inside will lead to lack of performance, anxiety, and overall failure. The best approach is to let go of all the negative thoughts and instead focus your energy on the positives.

I personally admire people who find a way to always look on the bright side of things especially when the going gets tough. And I've been lucky enough to have worked with such a guy. Daniel, an old colleague of mine, was one of those people that just radiated positivity. He was the best one to handle pressure situations at work and the only one who could finish last-minute project with positivity and success. If you hadn't known his story, you'd think that this guy has really figured out how to make things work.

So one day I asked him his secret of performing so well in crunch times. And his reply was simple: "That's just me man". He went on to describe how his childhood was tough and he had to earn his keep from the very beginning. His parents were divorced and his financial situation was tough. So from his early life he was conditioned to fight adversity because there was no other option. It was his will to fight off his hard life that helped him establish the habit to push through whatever obstacle life threw his way. By learning how to find a positive challenge and see the opportunity in every pressure moment, Daniel got to reap the benefits not only at work, but life in general.

The Perks of Weathering the Storm

Whenever we are faced with a tricky situation that we need to work harder to overcome – whether physically or mentally – we instantly tag it as a negative occurrence. But in fact, such occurrences are much needed for our emotional growth.

Think about your body for a second. In order for your muscles to grow stronger, they need to be challenged. Forcing your body to do push-ups or lift weighs may be uncomfortable, but physical exercise is the only way that will help you get stronger. This is called the *Principle of Progressive Resistance*, and it is based on the fact that your muscles have to work in order to grow, and that they will progressively overcome the resisting force.

What the gym is for your body, pressure situations are for your mind. We need to be tested, challenged and pushed to our limits in order to be able to get out of our comfort zones and thrive. The pressure situations are important for our emotional being-, but more important are the skills we acquire when rising to these situations.

Pressure Situations Help Us Develop Mental Toughness and Self Belief

The uncertain nature of pressure situations makes us work harder to achieve our goals. The fact that pressure situations produce this resisting force, leads to our inner fortitude. And the more we overcome such situations, the stronger and stronger we grow emotionally. This allows us to gain a psychological edge that helps us perform to our full potential when life throws these pressure occurrences our way. With each passing pressure moment you develop this enormous sense of self-belief that no matter what obstacle comes your way you will be able to get past it easily.

For instance, having an important exam will force you to work hard in order to pass it. By doing that, with every subsequent exam, you will become more mentally prepared for tackling such situations, as you will have an already established hard-working habit.

Another example can be of the racing legend Michael Schumacher. Anyone who watches Formula 1 knows the worst thing which can happen during a race is rain. But where his opponents used to crumble, Schumacher used to thrive with the belief that he is best racer in the world no matter what the conditions. That is what also earned him the title 'The Rainmaster'. And because of his mental strength, he was able to get through those challenges with flying colors.

Pressure Situations Enhance Creativity

When we are faced with a pressure situation, we are forced to unleash our creative-selves in order to come up with a way to overcome the occurrence. The pain that the challenge gives makes us tap into our creativity. Without the pressure situation in the first place, we would have never thought of such a creative way to solve the problem.

Take what happened with Apollo 13 in 1970 for example. On their way to the moon, the astronauts were faced with a threatening explosion that lead to a carbon dioxide buildup. In order to save the lives of the astronauts, NASA's scientists and engineers on ground joined forces and started brainstorming ideas on how to quickly solve the problem. They tried different set of materials and started putting together bits and pieces in order to come up with a model that could be easily replicated by the astronauts on board. They came up with something that was poorly-designed and ugly, but successful. Their under-pressure creativity actually saved 3 lives.

Your pressure situations can't be more dramatic than that and at the end of the day, they do force the creativity to meddle and save the day.

Pressure Situations Inspire Courage

It is in our nature to be more fearful than courageous. That's why we feel so uncomfortable when we are faced with pressure situations - because the uncertain outcome frightens us. But, once we come face to face with the heat, we are forced to come up with a solution. And that is what inspires us to find the courage and take the next step. This manifests in the form of a strong character and helps develop responsible behavior.

Captain Chesley Sullenberger's example here is worth sharing. Sullenberger or Sully as they call him, was carrying 155 passenger on a routine flight from New York to North Carolina, when things took a turn for the worse. A flock of geese went straight into the plane's engines causing both the engines of the aircraft to be disabled. In great pressure, Sully decided to land the aircraft on

Hudson River since it was the only surface which was smooth and large enough for landing. Thanks to Sully's courage, the plane landed safely without much impact.

Pressure Situations Keep Us Humble

High-pressure situations remind us that we are only human. We cannot plan everything, and we surely cannot predict every possible outcome. We have flaws and we make mistakes. These situations remind us that we are fragile, keeps us from becoming too prideful, and nurture our humble nature. And despite of the fact that some of us may see the light of the day when faced with pressure situations, there would have been quite a few instances throughout the journey in which if the luck hadn't gone our way, the outcome would have been very different.

Think about billionaires like Warren Buffet for a second. Warren Buffet has been living in the same house for the last 60 years eating the same breakfast every day. Why do you think people like him remain so humble and don't let success get to their head? It is actually because those adverse situations which remind them of their origins and make them realize even the most successful people have to go through a lot before being able to achieve what they eventually achieve.

Thriving in pressure situation gets you the most recognition

Achieving goals means overcoming many obstacles on your way there. When you work hard to accomplish something, you gain a deep appreciation for your achievements. The value of your achievements is measured by the outcome of the pressured performance you have to do. And pressure situations only make you value what you accomplish more.

Just think about this for a second. What do you think will get you more recognition at work? Something which was expected from you or something which nobody expected and believed you could achieve?

De-Stress Your Body and Mind

Now that we've established the importance of taking pressure positively, it is time to re-evaluate yourself and the feelings you have. Would you say that you are stressed in general? Have you lost your interest in work? Are you experiencing drop in confidence, irritability, increased anger, headaches, or fatigue during the day? If so, you need to take a healthy approach and knock down your stress levels in order for you to be able to turn pressure situations to your advantage.

By doing so, you will clear your path to understanding the true meaning of pressure situations in order to get in the right mindset and successfully tackle one. You cannot possibly turn something uncertain and uncomfortable into a positive challenge that can help you learn and grow if you go through your days with a negative attitude. If you are stressed out, you are most likely to have a negative outlook and think pessimistically about every tiny bump that you come across. By lowering your stress and welcoming a more positive mindset, you can then approach every situation more clearly, which is the only way in which you can possibly perform well.

Think of de-stressing yourself as the stepping stone at the beginning of your journey to learning how to thrive when under the gun.

Exercise

Just three 30-minute exercises per week can make a significant difference in the way you feel. You will knock down the blues, energize your body, and improve your overall cognitive function which is essential for handling pressure situations. By releasing endorphins that trigger positive feelings, regular exercise can definitely contribute to reducing the stress.

It doesn't have to be anything too challenging either. Jogging around the block, swimming, taking up a yoga class, joining up a gym or something as simple as hiking in nature can help you drag positivity back into your life.

Eat Balanced Meals

Eating nutritious and balanced meals is the key to reducing stress. Your body must be well-nourished in order to be able to cope not only to the side-effects of stress but also with the emotional demands of the pressure situations later on.

- Eat three balanced meals

- Make sure that breakfast is the most important meal of the day and never skip it

- Find the tie for healthy snacks such as a handful of nuts or an apple

- Ditch sugar and unhealthy food options

- Minimize the caffeine intake

Get Enough Sleep

Sleep does not only affect your mood, but also your memory, decision-making, and judgment, all of which are essential for scoring under pressure. In order to de-stress yourself and prepare your body and mind for handling pressure moments, you need to aim for a good night's sleep.

- Aim for 6-8 hours of sleep

- Try to go to bed and wake up the same time every day (even on the weekends)

- Have a cup of non-caffeinated tea before going to sleep

- Purge your electronics from your bedroom (or at least make sure they are on 'Mute') to ensure a good night's sleep

Organize Yourself

Make a to-do list with deadlines in order to make sure that your chores and obligations will be completed within a timely manner. Otherwise, you will just add more fuel to the fire and will feel more stressed. Place your to-do list somewhere you can easily see and access it (like your fridge), and stick to your schedule.

Surround Yourself with Positivity

Staying positive is extremely important in the process of decompressing and relieving yourself from stressful feelings. Here are some tips that can fill you up with good vibes:

- Have a massage from time to time

- Express gratitude and be thankful for the things you have

- Do not obsess with things you cannot control

- Cut ties with negative people

- Listen to relaxing music

- Have a relaxing bubble bath

- Meditate or do yoga

- Practice mindfulness

Secrets to Scoring Under Pressure

Living in such a high-paced world where everything we need is just a click of a button away, both our professional and personal lives are at constant pressure and become too demanding upon our mental resources. Regardless of the profession, status, or hobby, all of us face high-stake and uncertain situations where our emotional control is put to the test. But how many of us will rise and how many will crumble under pressure? What is that makes the difference between the regular and the super-successful individuals? Is it the fact that the latter can afford to play with fire? Or is it something else entirely?

Knowing not only how to cope but also thrive under pressure is a valuable, if not crucial skill that facilitates success in life. Having a healthy coping mechanism that will help you see past your fears and direct your performance toward a more satisfying outcome is essential for the competitive domains such as business, sport, the art of performing (think singers and actors), and life-depending situations (doctors, military people, etc.).

Exploring these skills and adapting them to improve your performance within heated situations – regardless of the domain - in your daily life, can help you gain healthy emotional control and train your mind to seek for the positivity in any occurrence.
Read on to learn the secrets to scoring under pressure.

Pre-empt & Anticipate

The best way you can condition yourself to excel under pressure is anticipate. Instead of letting things happen to you, anticipate and get them to work for you. Even though there are those in-the-spur-of-the-moment pressures that you simply cannot plan for, with the power of anticipation you will be able to successfully mitigate their negative impact. We are far more likely to succeed at performing a task when we are familiar with the occurrence that we are about to face. What anticipation does is it allows you to visualize whatever may lie ahead and then plan for your time and energy to be spent accordingly.

This is actually how athletes, surgeons, and militaries succeed. They plan their entire operation beforehand, thinking about all of the angles, going through all of the possible outcomes, and thinking of all the things that can go wrong in order to find the best way to avoid them.

For instance, to prepare for the Olympics, athletes spend a significant amount of time getting familiar with all the things that can distract them during their performance such as the lighting, the acoustics, or the overall feel of the moment. You need to be on top of everything and know exactly what to expect.

By visualizing and preparing yourself for the worse-case scenario, you ensure that when the situation demands you to act a certain way you are fully prepared. Ask yourself a bunch of what-if questions and it will help you to avoid getting startled by the intensity of any situation because in your head, you already know how all the scenes play out it.

Practice to avoid being overwhelmed with pressure

No matter what you do, pressure will keep following you. And it doesn't really care whether you are prepared for it or not or whether you perceive it as an opportunity or as a threat. So why not deal with it head on?

Most of the time, mistakes are made because we are preoccupied with the importance of the task at hand. The more important the moment is, the more pressure we feel and the higher the chance for failure. Here, the pressure distorts the perceptions, leading to the impairment of our cognitive abilities such as judgment and decision-making. By minimalizing the importance of the moment, you can actually avoid this distortion and help yourself perform in a much more organized manner.

One effective way of reducing the perceived intensity of a situation is practice. If you are able to practice and make yourself go through more and more of such situations, chances are with time, you will be able to tame your fear and make it work in your favor (as a means of a kick you need to initiate something). Start with small tasks, like for example cleaning your desk. Give yourself a certain time limit to do it. This will help you to familiarize yourself with the uncertainties that come with such time-limited situations in the future.

To further prove my point, let me ask you something. Who do you think of these people is under the most pressure?

A soccer player getting ready for a free kick.

A person sewing her friend's wedding dress for the first time

An architect involved in constructing a building.

When you think about it, it is the person who is sewing the dress for her friend who is under the most pressure. You see, regardless of the fact that this is the least meaningful task, that person feels the most pressure because she is afraid of failure the most. The soccer player is prepared for such occurrence, the architect is also trained to see the construction as "just another building to construct" and perform the task almost automatically, but for this person, afraid that she might not rise to the occasion, this may be the most meaningful dress she has ever made.

It's One of Many Opportunities

Whether it is the most important job interview you've ever had or working on the most important project for a huge client, some pressure situations seem like they are one-in-a-lifetime moments. But the truth is, they are not. That is the system of life. As long as you keep yourself in the game, you will have plenty of more, often far better opportunities to conquer and prove your mettle to the world.

In the book "Performing Under Pressure – The Science of Doing Your Best When It Matters the Most", Hendrie Weisinger and J.P. Pawliw-Fry talk about a study performed on auto mechanics. One group of auto mechanics were asked to assemble an engine and told that if done correctly, they would become candidates for a supervisory position. The same task was given to another group of auto mechanics, but the second group was also told that if they were to make a mistake, they'd be given other opportunities to try again. Who do you think performed better? The first group was under a lot of pressure thinking that this was that one big shot and made more mistakes than the second group who approached the task as one of many opportunities.

Another example worth sharing is of the renowned professional boxer, Michael Bentt. Bentt never considered himself a professional boxer. He was forced by his father to enter the sport from a young age and despite the fact that he had a few long undefeated streaks, he never felt boxing was his main forte. And when he had to defend his Heavyweight Championship title for the first time, he lost, by Knock Out. Now for any boxer a loss by Knock Out is a big deal. But to make it worse, Bentt was taken to the hospital after the fight and was told he would never be able to fight again because of a severe injury to his head during the fight.

That would have taken out the gas from a lot of people, but that didn't stop Bentt to live his life to the fullest. In fact opportunities came in and he was able to pursue his career in something he actually had some interest; writing and acting. He was casted in Muhammad Ali's biopic *Ali* and has continued his work as a writer and an actor.

So do not think of the faced pressure situation as one-of-a-kind. It is realistic to think that many other opportunities will be thrown your way. Approaching the situation with this mindset will help you depressurize the moment and focus on giving a good performance.

Have clarity of thought

Your heart is pounding fast, your breath is shortened, and your palms are sweating. Everything depends solely on how you approach the situation. But you're unsure if the path you are thinking to take will lead to success or will it result in the same bad outcome you got previously.

When we think too much about our past or our future negatively, we jeopardize our chances of success in the present. We allow stress to mount on ourselves by letting negative thoughts creep up. With a lack of clarity in thought, we struggle to focus on one thing and let doubts get the better of us. And when the time comes and the pressure rises, we are nowhere near the ideal state of mind necessary to strike when it matters the most.

That is why, during crunch times it is imperative to have a clear mind with only our goals to focus on. The trick here is to prioritize. List down all the important tasks and give them weight according to their importance. Start with the most important one and further break it down to actionable objectives. And when you are in the process of pursuing those objectives, let everything else fade away. Build your power to ignore. With time and practice, you will be able use this trick on demand.

To give you some context, I'll take an example of a research. This study was conducted to know why people perceive sports teams who play on their home turf to have a slight "home advantage" as compared to the visiting team. One conclusion drawn was that the pressure which the home crowds mount on the referee and the overall environment of the stadium may force him to get distracted and subconsciously give a few calls in favor of the home team. On the contrary, a similar study also suggested that sometimes the home team also crumbles under pressure thanks to the expectations from the home crowd of performing out of their skins.

Another trick to have a clear mind is to engage in some pep talk or delve in thoughts which lets you turn on your "Game Mode". Every time you feel you are under pressure or at the brink of doing something immensely important, talk to yourself or engage in some activity which reminds you to be on top of your game.

This is what Michael Phelps, the champion Olympian used to do just before starting any race. He used to engage in a small activity of listening to Young Jeezy or Eminem while stepping on and off of his starting block just to ensure that he is all pepped up to focus on what mattered the most at that particular time.

Focus on the Process, not the Outcome

Many times, we fancy the outcome so much that the process of achieving it gets blurred. We do not think about the difficulties we need to go through to achieve the said objective. Only the glory of the outcome is perceived. And when a person wrongfully engages in a task trying to pursue the outcome, the minute details and small hiccups along the way prove to be a source of pressure mounting on the person. We need to ensure that we are ready for all small or big challenges and are well aware of the process in order to achieve the objective.

By focusing on what the mission is and not on what the mission will lead to, you will release the pressure of the situation in three ways:

- You will avoid getting distracted and stay on track

- Will stay anchored at the moment and recognize the best way to perform the task

Take for example, a figure skater. She has set a goal for winning a medal in an important competition. In order to be successful, however, instead of focusing on the prize, she gives great attention to her quad jump and elements within it to make a successful landing. She carefully studies the condition and prepares accordingly to develop a 'winning attitude'.

Avoid Comparison and Remember Past Successes

Most people fail to shine in high-pressure situations because they are overwhelmed by the success of others and don't give themselves enough chance. They wrongly feel others have achieved so much more than them and have a "catch-up" mentality thinking their own performance cannot be up to par. This is "self-inflicted pressure" where you're in such a mentality that you will always lag behind.

What these people don't realize is the fact that everyone in this world is different and have their own story to tell. Even the brightest of the performers have their daily struggles if not major ones. But what keeps them apart is their ability to know that they were able to get through those struggles in the past and the future should be no exception. The trick here is to not compare yourself with someone else, but rather with your own best self. And as long as you are on that path, you should remind yourself that you are doing okay.

Also, the memories we have of our past experiences are imprinted in our brains, and the more we think about them, the stronger their impact becomes. Visiting your past successful self can also give you a real confidence boost that you crave during pressure moments. Visualizing what you managed to achieve in the past will give you the much-needed nudge in order to realize that, once you did it right, you can do it again. Reminiscing on your past trophies may be just what you need to tackle the given task with confidence.

Not sure you can do it? Try this exercise whenever you are in a pressure situation and see how helpful this can be:

- Write down all the times that you managed to perform with success in pressure situations.

- Have a comfortable seat and make sure to take deep breaths to regulate the breathing.

- Try to really picture these past moments. *How did it feel when your boss gave you that promotion?* Think of all of your senses to relieve the experience, the sounds, smells, sights.

- Say "I was successful". I did it".

- Repeat this simple exercise for as long as it takes until it becomes a habit to flash back to past successes whenever you are faced with a pressure situation.

Under Pressure at your workplace? Use these tips:

Although pressure situations can be found pretty much in every aspect of our lives, they are especially common in the workplace. Regardless of your job - whether you are used to working in a high-stress environment such as combat area or you deliver mail for a living - at some point, you are bound to face some real pressure at work.

Managing that pressure is paramount not only for getting through the workday but for thriving and moving upward as well.

And while all of the previously mentioned techniques can help you perform better when faced with work pressure, here are some tips that can be especially beneficial in the process of de-pressurizing the heated moments at work.

Take Breaks

This is a no-brainer, really. Many times you cannot see clearly mainly because your head is one giant mess. Whenever you see the frustration piling up, just hit the 'reset' button when possible. Taking a few 15-minute breaks during your workday can help your focus stay sharp, which will allow you to approach your pressure situations with the right mindset.

Some workplaces will not allow you longer breaks. If that is the case, just use whatever you can. Even getting up to 5-minutes break can be beneficial. Go refill your water bottle, step outside to take a few deep breaths, or go to the bathroom to sit in quiet and close your eyes for a few moments.

This can be especially helpful when working on huge projects when your mind is supposed to stay sharp. By taking quick breaks you will be able to energize your mind and get rid of the feeling of overwhelmed which will help you work longer and much more productively.

Oprah Winfrey for example says she goes to a quiet place like a bathroom cubicle to relax close her eyes and breathe whenever she feels the pressure of getting a good show on the air.

Approach the Situation as a Game

This may seem silly, but who doesn't like playing games? Slaying dragons or defeating evil witches are both fun ways to approach the completion of tasks. The point here is to find something that will keep the pressure at bay and make the whole performance more fun. Need to complete an important project? Think that each task you complete takes you one step closer to defeating the enemy. Once you've delivered the project – you have won and slayed the dragon. Whatever motivates you to stay focused on the task at hand and do not feel pressure, feel free to use it.

Imagine that your boss is breathing down your neck. He has just assigned a huge project that requires of you to complete several different task, but doesn't quite think you can make it. Think of your boss as a dragon and of each task as the step that gets you closer to the final level. With each completed task, you are a step closer to slaying the dragon. By completing your project, you slay the dragon and win. You show your boss that you can actually do great work.

Share

The next time you feel the pressure of the upcoming project, deadline, or presentation piling up, share your thoughts with your colleague, peer, or your boss. This will not only give you support and an emotional boost, but you will also be relieved to know that the others may also feel the same way, and you may even contribute to a collective motivation. It is easy to discuss the pressure you are feeling with someone when the stakes are high for everyone.

Even if the stakes are high just for you individually, feel free to reach to someone for assistance. Asking for help or sharing your thoughts with a trusted coworker may be just what you need to get things done smoothly.

The next time you feel the work pressure take a toll over your performance, go to the coworker you trust the most and share your feelings with them, Sharing your feelings is probably the best way to overcome an issue. Why do you think therapists are for? By discussing the pressure you are feeling with someone and getting things off of your chest, you can have the situation analyzed from a different point of view. Which sometimes is just what it takes for the task to be completed with success.

Give your best but let Go of Perfectionism

If your standards are really high, the pressure of the situation may be just in your head. So, what should you do when you are given a project? Aim for a *done* project where you believe you have put enough effort, not a *perfect* project. Of course, this shouldn't sacrifice the quality of your work, but you shouldn't preoccupy yourself with giving your 100 percent on every task.

When you give more focus to putting good efforts rather than perfectly executing a task, you are allowing yourself to control the controllable. However if you are of the perception that everything needs to go smoothly without any hiccups, you let fear come in to play because all your focus is on avoiding failure due to which ultimately pressure gets the best of you.

The next time your boss assigns you a project, even if it is important, try to think of it as something that you are volunteering for, something where the expectation bar is pretty low. Approaching situations this way may help you let go of your need to prove everyone that you are the best, and may actually turn out to be just the tool you need to provide your best work after all.

Learn to say "No"

Some pressure situations are such where you need to analyze and foresee if it can be avoided. This is because these situations can be a cause of unwanted pressure mounting on yourself. Your mental and emotional faculties can only handle so much of burden and it is best to channel all your efforts, energy and capabilities towards which matters most to you at the time.

If you are used to saying "Yes" all the time and committed to helping your coworkers even when you are in over your head with your own projects, you may want to reconsider this habit of yours. Be realistic about your time and make sure to get your priorities straight. What is more important? To finish the project you are already late for or to help your colleague finish his and miss your deadline? Be polite, but firm with your answer. Make sure that your colleagues know that you have strong boundaries.

The next time your colleague asks you for your helping hand and you are clearly nowhere near done with your own work, say something like: "I am really sorry Sarah, but I am running against the clock with this Parker project. Maybe John can be of assistance?"

Be organized to tackle pressure with preparedness

Sometimes, your lack of organization is only to blame. If you are unorganized, it is easy to forget an upcoming deadline or to constantly be racing against the time. Make sure to use your calendar and know what your priorities are.

Also, try not to juggle too many things at once. Working on one project at a time will keep your mind focused and will definitely yield in a more productive performance. If it is your boss who is assigning projects you cannot possibly finish on time, share your thoughts with them.

Here are some tips that will help you stay organized at the office:

- Keep your desk clean

- Have your schedule written in your calendar

- Keep your calendar visible at all times

- Write down the top priorities for each day

- Use sticky notes and write down the things you don't want to forget

Handling Pressure Situation like a Boss – Cheat Sheet

As you can see, being on top of things and thriving in those heated moments is indeed possible if you are armed with the right knowledge. With simple steps and techniques, you can turn around even the most impossible situation to your advantage.

Keep in Mind that Pressure Situations are Beneficial. Pressure situations shouldn't be perceived as negative as they challenge you to become better. They improve your cognitive function, build up your confidence, make you more humble, help you appreciate your achievements, instill courageousness, etc.

De-Stress Your Body. If you are under stress, you may not be able to succeed at handling pressure as you are probably used to perceiving every little inconvenience like the end of the world. Let go of the need to control everything, eat well, exercise regularly, sleep well, and do things that relax you and fill you up with positivity.

Perform Well Under Pressure. Make sure to use all of the techniques for turning pressure situations into challenges in order to blossom:

- Perceive them as opportunities

- Reduce the importance of the pressure moment

- Get prepared for unexpected twists and turns

- Keep in mind that the pressure situation is not your only opportunity

- Focus on the actual performance not the outcome

- Remember the times you were successful in the past

Handle Work Pressure Well. Use these tips to be able to cut down the feelings of negative pressure at work and to actually use that pressure to perform even better:

- Take regular breaks and be organized.

- Think of pressure situations as games

- Share your feelings with others

- Stay focused on your project and learn how to say "no"

Conclusion

Congratulations! You are but a step away from turning every pressure situation into an opportunity for you to learn, grow, and rise to the top. The next thing you need to do is to simply take advantage of all the secrets and tips from this book, and see them work magic the next time you are faced with a pressure situation.

This book may not be able to change the pressure that you feel at given moments, but by providing you with useful techniques and an approach that the most successful people in the world use, you can surely find a way to be effective when the heat piles up.

Even though it was short, I have given my best for the tips and strategies included in this book to be as up-to-the-point and as relevant as possible, in order to lay out the foundation of your performance under pressure. Using them to your advantage will not only help you learn, but successfully grow as well.

Now, get ready to accept the opportunities that life throws your way and watch yourself thrive!

Did you find this book helpful? Leave an honest <u>review</u> *and let others know! Your feedback will be greatly appreciated.*

Thank you!